THE MENACE OF
AIDS

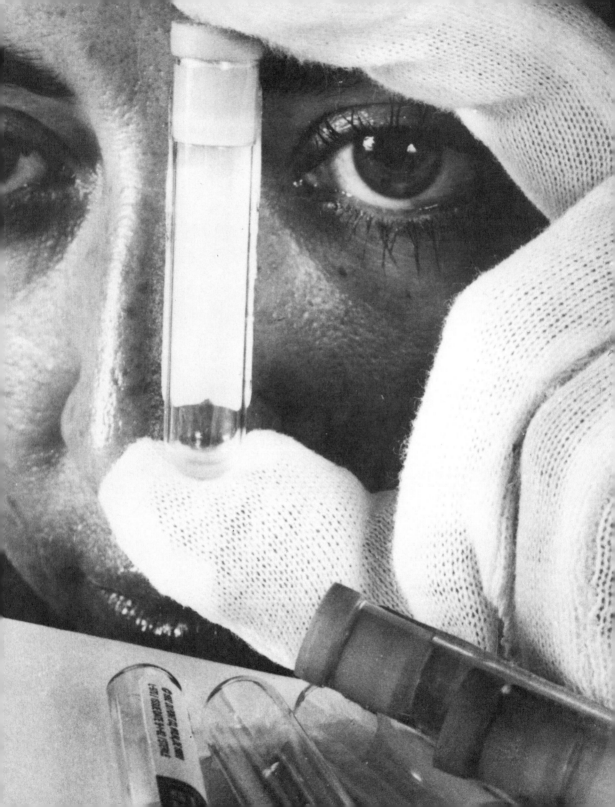

THE MENACE OF AIDS

A SHADOW ON OUR LAND

DOUGLAS A. EAGLES

FRANKLIN WATTS
NEW YORK|LONDON|TORONTO|SYDNEY|1988
A FIRST BOOK

Frontis: *a technologist at one of Du Pont's quality control laboratories in Wilmington, Delaware, examines a tube to be used by other laboratories for the isolation of microbes in the blood of AIDS victims.*

Photographs courtesy of:
AP/Wide World Photos: pp. 2, 13, 14 (top), 18, 26, 37, 48 (inset), 57, 62, 64; UPI/Bettmann Newsphotos: pp. 14 (bottom), 33, 48, 61; Photo Researchers, Inc.: p. 29 (Dr. A. Liepins), 43 (CNRI/SPL); CDC: pp. 39, 45, 66.

Library of Congress Cataloging in Publication Data
Eagles, Douglas A.
The menace of AIDS : a shadow on our land / Douglas Eagles.
p.   cm. — (A First book)
Bibliography: p.
Includes index.
Summary: Discusses the origins, causes, characteristics, methods of infection, possible cures and prevention, and social aspects of the deadly disease.
ISBN 0-531-10567-9
1. AIDS (Disease)—Juvenile literature.   [1. AIDS (Disease)]
I. Title. II. Series.
RC607.A26E33   1988
616.97'92—dc 19   88-16983 CIP AC

CONTENTS

THE MENACE OF
AIDS

PREFACE

A NASTY
BEGINNING

The first time this author heard about AIDS was late in 1981. The first time he heard a detailed description of the disease was early in 1982, at a lecture given by a physician. The purpose of the lecture was to alert other physicians and scientists to a disturbing new disease.

After a brief introduction, the speaker began discussing a series of color slides he had brought, showing people who had come to a clinic in New York City complaining of a variety of problems. Some had no specific complaint. They just didn't feel well and frequently ran high fevers. One slide showed what the physician saw when he peered into the eyeball of one patient. In the back of the eye, easily seen on the surface of the retina (the part of the eye that detects light), was a cluster of swollen, bright-red blood vessels. The physician said that this was a symptom of a condition known as Kaposi's sarcoma, a type of cancer. The patient also had an infection. The infection was treated with antibiotics, and the patient was sent home. Two weeks later, this same patient was back, complaining of fevers, difficulty in breathing, and generally not feeling well. He was found to have pneumonia, and inspection of his eyes showed that the cluster of swollen blood vessels seen earlier had nearly tripled in size. He was admitted to the hospital for treatment of his pneumonia and for evaluation of his other symptoms. The sequence of events that followed was a frustrating one for the physician and patient. No sooner would one infection be cleared up than another would develop. Each infection would progress with unusual speed, as though the patient had no ability to fight disease on his own. Meanwhile, his Kaposi's sarcoma rapidly grew worse, and he lost the sight in both eyes. The patient eventually died, overwhelmed by multiple infections and cancer.

In the meantime, other patients had come into the hospital, complaining of a variety of ailments. These often included swelling in the neck and under the arms. Also, many of the infections involved organisms that are always present in humans but that rarely cause problems.

All of the patients seen in this one hospital did have some features in common. All were young homosexual men (men who have sexual relations with other men) and all showed very little resistance to disease. Some were intravenous drug users. (Intravenous means "injecting something into the vein." In this case, we are referring to the use of illegal drugs.) These people were among the first in the United States to have AIDS (acquired immune deficiency syndrome). All of them have since died.

CHAPTER

1

A PUZZLING
NEW DISEASE

ORIGINS OF AIDS

The year 1981 is usually taken as the starting date for AIDS in the United States. That was the year in which the disease was first recognized. The earliest cases that fit the AIDS pattern were seen in 1979, although there is some evidence that a person who died in the United States in 1972 had the disease. Some have even suggested that AIDS might have been around for as long as a hundred years.

Where did AIDS come from? Obviously, this is a question of great interest to scientists studying the disease and to physicians treating it.

Sometimes, "new" diseases are just new to us. They have been around for some time but have been confined to other countries. In such countries, often developing ones, there are many poor people who have inadequate food, housing, and medical care. Because people in the more developed countries of North America, Europe,

Asia, and Australia rarely come into contact with these people, diseases among them may not be recognized for a long time. Sometimes, however, brand-new diseases develop.

The current epidemic of AIDS appears to have originated in central Africa. It is not certain how the disease started there. A disease very much like AIDS has been found in one species of monkey called the green monkey. Human AIDS might somehow have started from this disease. The route from Africa to the United States appears to have involved a group of men from Haiti who went to central Africa to work. The men probably contracted the disease from men or women there and brought it back to Haiti when they returned home. It appears that it came to the United States in the late 1970s, when a group of homosexual men from California visited Haiti on vacation. When it first appeared in the United States, AIDS was found almost exclusively among male homosexuals.

Recently, it has been discovered that the AIDS virus is present in some mosquitoes in Africa. This has led to some concern that it might be spread by mosquito bites, as are malaria and some other diseases. There is no evidence yet, however, that anyone has ever gotten AIDS from mosquito bites.

WHAT CAUSES AIDS?

You have probably heard something about AIDS already. It is frequently in the news. We are all going to hear even more about it in the future, and it is likely to affect the lives of all of us, even if we do not become ill with it ourselves.

a mother and infant
green monkey

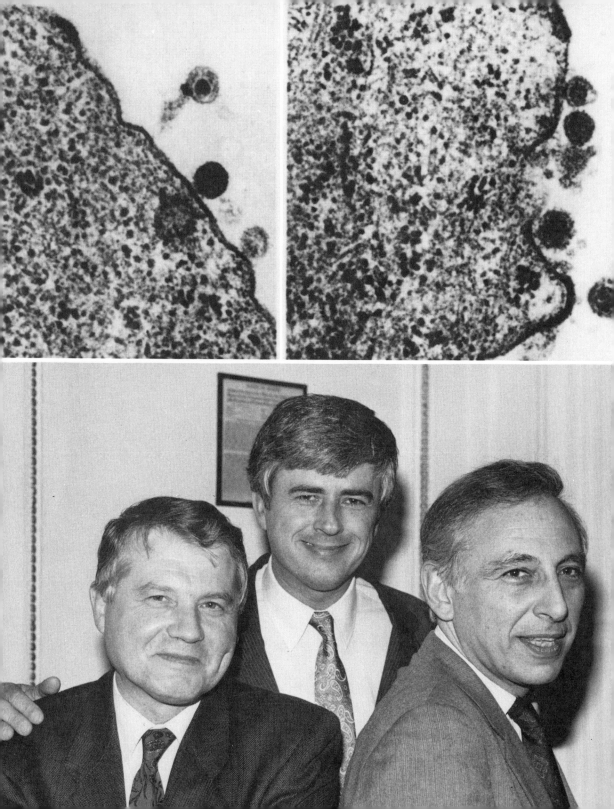

The purpose of this book is to provide some facts about the disease. This book is written for young people, even though young people are the ones least likely to get or have AIDS right now. AIDS must be of concern to all of us. Part of the goal of this book is to provide information that will help you avoid getting this disease later.

Fortunately, it is not that easy to get AIDS. Unfortunately, once a person has the disease, the chances of survival are zero. So far, everyone who has been found to have full-blown AIDS (we will explain this shortly) has died within two years of being diagnosed. So far, there is no vaccine (see next chapter) to protect people against AIDS, and there is no cure. Therefore, it is very important for all of us to take some simple precautions that can almost guarantee protection from getting this terrible disease.

It is now generally agreed that AIDS is caused by a virus that is now known as *HIV* (human immunodeficiency virus). In the United States, the virus was first called HTLV-III (human T-lymphotropic virus type III) and in Europe it was called LAV (lymphadenopathy-

Top: the AIDS viruses identified by Drs. Gallo and Montagnier. Bottom: Luc Montagnier (left) of the Pasteur Institute and Robert Gallo (right) of the National Cancer Institute, co-discoverers of the AIDS virus. In between them is Myron Essex, a professor of virology and chairman of the Department of Cancer Biology at the Harvard School of Public Health. Essex is another highly regarded AIDS researcher.

associated virus). Two names were used to identify the virus because two laboratories identified it at about the same time and each gave it a different name. In the United States, Dr. Robert Gallo of the National Cancer Institute (part of the National Institutes of Health) led the way. In Europe, the work was carried out by Dr. Luc Montagnier and his team at the Pasteur Institute in Paris, France.

We now assume that HTLV-III and LAV are identical, though we may never be sure, since the virus appears to have many different forms and seems capable of changing form quite often, just like the virus that causes the common cold. Research workers throughout the world today use the term HIV to identify the AIDS virus.

STAGES AND
SYMPTOMS OF AIDS

What happens when a person gets AIDS? Most scientists agree that there are at least three stages in the disease. In the very earliest part of the first stage, a person is infected with the virus but shows no symptoms at all. This is common for many diseases. After a short period, usually only a few weeks or months, the immune system manages to produce some antibodies to the virus. The blood of the infected person begins to show the presence of AIDS antibodies. (In a few cases, however, it may not be possible to detect the presence of these antibodies for as long as a year.) Antibodies are chemicals—actually, blood proteins—produced by the body in response to an infection. They are one of a number of defenses that our bodies have for protecting us from disease.

We produce antibodies whenever a foreign substance or germ "invades" the body. A different type of antibody is produced for each different kind of infection. This is how it is possible to find out if a person has had a certain type of infection. Often a person who has been infected with the AIDS virus and is producing antibodies has no other symptoms of disease. It is at this stage that the disease can usually first be identified. A blood test can determine whether or not the antibody is present. If the blood contains antibodies against the AIDS virus, it means that the virus has entered the body.

Sometimes the test does not detect any antibody in an infected person, usually because the infection is too recent. The body has not yet had time to make enough antibodies to be detected. Unfortunately, it is in this period, whether or not the person is producing antibodies, that the infected person is most likely to accidentally pass the virus on to another person.

No one is sure what happens next in the course of the disease. Usually, a person who is infected with AIDS does not develop any other symptoms for at least several years after the infection. In fact, at the time of this writing, it appears that people are more likely to develop symptoms of AIDS more than five years after the infection than they are in the first five years. The virus appears to remain in the body in a dormant (inactive) state. Some investigators have found evidence that the virus resides in the Langerhans cells, cells of the immune system found in the skin, but it is too early to be sure that this is the important reservoir of dormant AIDS virus particles.

The second stage of the disease is called *ARC* (AIDS-related complex). A person may be infected with the virus for as long as ten years before showing this second stage. For all of this time, he or she may be infecting other people.

The first symptom of ARC is swollen lymph nodes. Lymph nodes are structures in the body where white blood cells collect; for example, they can be found in the neck and underarms. White blood

Abbott HTLV III EIA Screening Test
Positive Result

HTLV III Recombinant Confirmatory Test
Positive Result

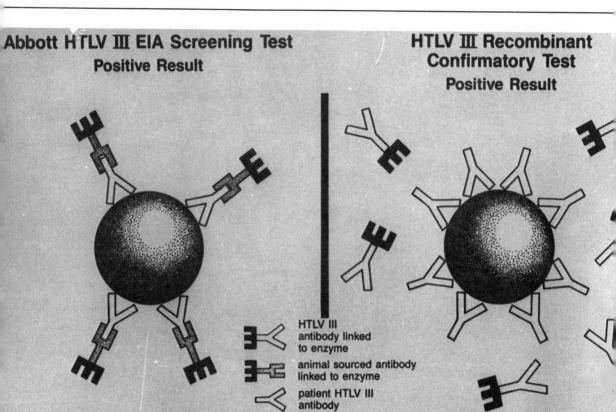

HTLV III antibody linked to enzyme

animal sourced antibody linked to enzyme

patient HTLV III antibody

The HTLV III screening test uses a sandwich principle to detect HTLV antibodies. When present in a blood sample, the patient HTLV III antibody binds to HTLV III viral proteins coated on the bead. The sandwich is formed when antibody (animal sourced) linked to an enzyme latches on to the antibody from the patient sample. The presence of enzyme is then measured optically using a spectrophotometer. The more antibody present in the sample, the more enzyme that will be bound to the bead and the greater the intensity of the color that will be read.

The confirmatory test uses a competitive assay principle. In this case, antibody from the patient sample competes with enzyme-linked antibody in the reagents to bind with HTLV III viral proteins coated on the bead. These proteins are produced via recombinant DNA (rDNA) technology. The purity of these proteins assures that only HTLV III antibody in the patient sample can displace the enzyme-linked antibody to produce a positive result. In the confirmatory test, a positive result is measured by the lack of color intensity.

screening tests for AIDS

cells are important in fighting infection. The original European term for the virus (*lymphadenopathy*-associated virus) refers to the tumorlike growth of these lymph nodes in the course of the disease. Additional symptoms may include loss of appetite, loss of weight, fever, night sweats, diarrhea, tiredness, and low resistance to infection. All of these are a part of the condition called ARC, but many of these symptoms are also found in other diseases. In general, these are also symptoms of AIDS, but they are more severe when they occur in AIDS.

The third stage of the disease is full-blown AIDS, or, more simply, AIDS. AIDS can only be properly diagnosed by a qualified medical person, but its symptoms include those listed under ARC above and may include a persistent cough and fever and difficulty in breathing. Often, people with these symptoms are found to have a particular form of pneumonia *(Pneumocystis carinii).* Some people may have the condition discussed earlier, Kaposi's sarcoma. This is a disease of the connective tissue. Connective tissue is found throughout the body. It holds cells together to form organs such as the heart and liver. In Kaposi's sarcoma it is the connective tissue in the lining of the blood vessels (arteries and veins) that is affected. As the disease progresses, numerous purple-colored blotches and bumps appear on the skin. Most importantly, the body's immune system is badly weakened. This is what the term "immune deficiency" means. A person with AIDS is no longer able to withstand infections. People with AIDS do not die because of the direct effects of the virus. They die of diseases that they would ordinarily not get, or which they might get but would not ordinarily find life-threatening, such as chicken pox.

If they do not die of such diseases, they usually die of cancer, especially Kaposi's sarcoma. Interestingly, Kaposi's sarcoma, when it occurs by itself, is rarely life-threatening. It becomes a serious problem only when a person's defenses are weakened by the AIDS virus.

What exactly happens in the body when a person develops AIDS? It is known that when AIDS develops, the AIDS virus (HIV) infects the helper T cells (see next chapter). It multiplies within these cells, destroys them, and is released to infect other helper T cells. As the helper T cells are destroyed, the body cannot fight either the AIDS virus or other infections. This seems to be why people with AIDS are plagued by infections of yeast and bacteria that are usually present in our environment all the time but that rarely cause illness. It also appears to be why people with AIDS suffer from rapidly spreading cancers. Normally, the immune system attacks cancer cells when they occur in the body, just as it does infectious organisms. AIDS is a disease that attacks the very mechanism we use to fight disease. This is why it is so serious.

People who develop this third stage of the disease, full-blown AIDS, die. Death usually occurs within two years of the time this stage is diagnosed. The amount of time that passes between the second stage (ARC) and the third stage (AIDS) varies but may be several years.

SOME ESTIMATES

How many of the people who become infected with the AIDS virus develop the third stage of the disease (AIDS)? We don't know for sure. The earliest estimates were that about 10 to 20 percent of infected persons would develop AIDS. Unfortunately, more recent (1986) estimates suggest that from 20 to 50 percent of the people who are infected with the virus will develop AIDS within five years.

In other words, we now think that a very large fraction of the people who become infected with the virus will die from it. The most recent estimates are that there are about 1.5 million people in the United States infected with the AIDS virus right now, and that approximately 180,000 of these people will die of AIDS by 1991.

WILL THERE BE A
VACCINE OR CURE?

What are the chances that science will come up with a vaccine or a cure for AIDS? We really don't know. Let's consider the vaccine question first.

Many investigators are very pessimistic about finding a useful vaccine against AIDS. The reason is that, like most viruses, including the ones that cause the common cold, the AIDS virus appears to exist in many different forms. It is even thought that the virus may change into many different forms within the body of a single infected person. As we will see in our discussion of vaccination in the next chapter, for a vaccine to work it must mimic the agent it is used to protect against. This is because immune responses are very specific. Protection against one virus does not insure protection against even a closely related virus. In order to protect against AIDS, it will be necessary to find some part of the virus that is common to all AIDS viruses and to which the immune system can react. A troubling question for those pursuing a vaccine is why the immune system first produces antibodies to the virus and then seems to tolerate the presence of the virus for so many years.

The short-term prospects for developing a cure for AIDS, or at least a way to treat its symptoms, seem somewhat better. These are based upon the recent development of drugs that appear to interfere with the reproduction of the virus. *AZT* (azidothymidine, or zidovudine) is the most common drug now being used to treat people with AIDS and the only one that really seems to improve the condition of most of the people receiving it. It is also the only drug currently approved by the Food and Drug Administration for the treatment of AIDS.

Some patients on AZT show increased resistance to infections, and they recover some of their lost weight. However, AZT may interfere with the production of some types of blood cells. Clinical trials have also recently begun in Europe on an antibiotic, but it is still too early to tell if either this drug or AZT will be truly effective or have serious side effects. The certainty of death for people with AIDS, however, makes any drug that shows positive results worth trying. It is hoped that these or other drugs will prove useful in fighting this terrible disease and help humankind to avert the loss of millions of lives in the next few years. For now, however, our best hope lies with limiting the spread of the AIDS virus in the population.

CHAPTER
2

THE IMMUNE SYSTEM

If you had superhuman vision, you would see that the air you breathe, the water you drink, many of the foods you eat, your own skin, and the skin of the members of your family, your friends, and your pets all have large numbers of organisms on them. Many of these are harmless and do not cause disease. Some, however, can cause disease if they are able to enter your body and establish an infection.

Most of us, during the course of a normal day, are exposed to a large number of bacteria, yeasts, fungi, viruses, and other kinds of infectious agents that all have the potential to cause disease. If we are confronted with such a large array of diseases on a daily basis, why is it that we become ill so rarely? Many people, for example, go for years without ever missing a day of school or work because of illness.

The part of our bodies that is mostly responsible for our resistance to this barrage of disease-producing agents in our midst is called the *immune system*. The immune system does not have a central organ associated with it, like the circulatory system (the heart) and the nervous system (the brain). Instead, it consists of large numbers of cells scattered throughout the body. In general, the cells of this very important system are produced and mature in a few separate places—for example, the central regions of bones, called the *bone marrow,* and a gland called the *thymus.* They are distributed throughout the body by the blood in the circulatory system or by another set of vessels called the *lymphatic system.*

Antigens are substances that are foreign to the body and that produce a response by the body's immune system. One such response is the production of blood proteins called *antibodies.* When antibodies combine with antigens in the blood, they "neutralize" the antigens; that is, they make them harmless. This is just one type of immune response. If this response is successful and overcomes the invading organisms, then the person recovers from the disease. Often, this response is so effective that we are not even aware that we were threatened with disease. On the other hand, if the immune system fails to neutralize disease-producing organisms, then we may become seriously ill.

Physicians often prescribe *antibiotics,* which are drugs that kill the type of organism causing the disease. Usually, people would recover from the disease anyway, but the use of an antibiotic speeds recovery so that people feel better sooner.

In many countries, people are *vaccinated* shortly after they are born. Vaccinations protect people against certain infectious diseases, such as measles, smallpox, and polio. Because these diseases can be serious, and because they can spread rapidly from person to person, routine vaccination of all people is one way of protecting a population. Vaccination against smallpox has been so successful that there has not been a single case, worldwide, re-

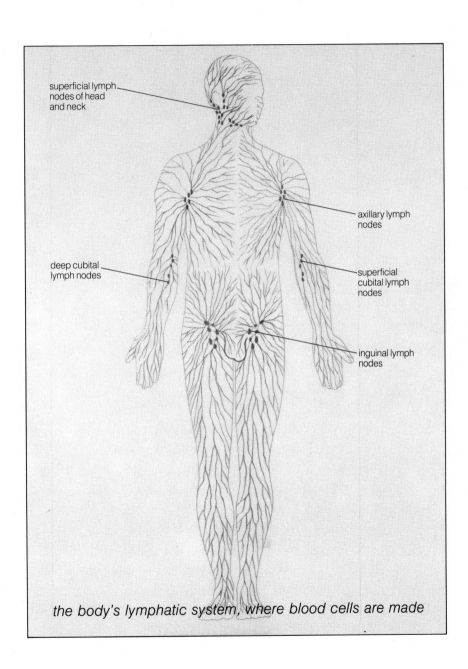

superficial lymph
nodes of head
and neck

axillary lymph
nodes

deep cubital
lymph nodes

superficial
cubital lymph
nodes

inguinal lymph
nodes

the body's lymphatic system, where blood cells are made

smallpox vaccinations being given at New York City Public Health Department headquarters after a Canadian boy on a visit to New York in August 1962 exhibited the disease

ported in the past ten years. It is likely that this once-fatal disease has been totally eliminated.

The way in which vaccinations work is fairly simple. The organism that causes the disease is first identified. Then large numbers of it are grown in the laboratory. The organisms are then usually killed, often by heating them, and are used to produce a vaccine. The organisms, though dead, will still contain the same antigens that the live ones had.

When the dead viruses are injected into the blood, the immune system will respond to them as though the organisms were still alive. There are at least two parts to this response. The first is that the appropriate antibody will be produced by the body. The second is that the cells that produce that antibody will multiply. The antibody will then attack the antigen on the dead organism, eventually causing it to be removed from the body. But some of the antibody-producing cells will remain in the person's body for the rest of his or her life. Then, at some later time, if the live organism infects the body, the body will be ready for it. The cells that produce that antibody will spring into action, releasing chemicals that will attack the organism. These same cells will also begin to multiply rapidly, resulting in large amounts of new antibody being produced. The invading organism will be overwhelmed before it can produce serious disease.

Sometimes live organisms are used in vaccines, but they have been changed slightly so that they do not produce the disease. Vaccines that have been produced against polio illustrate the two types. The first polio vaccine, produced by Dr. Jonas Salk, consisted of a killed polio virus. The second, produced by Dr. Albert Sabin, was a harmless live virus. Both were so effective in protecting people against infection that polio almost disappeared. Unfortunately, believing that the danger of polio was past, people stopped taking these vaccines. Thus the disease has not yet been completely eradicated.

All of this seems simple enough, but we might ask the question: How does the immune system manage to attack only foreign agents and not the many different cell types found in our own bodies? In fact, for some unfortunate people, the immune system does sometimes make this kind of mistake. The diseases that result are called *autoimmune diseases*. A disease called myasthenia gravis, which involves weakness in the muscles, and some types of arthritis are examples of autoimmune diseases. But in most instances the immune system works as it should. How?

There are many different types of cells in the immune system, and we cannot consider them all here. One of the most important types is the *lymphocyte*. There are two general kinds of lymphocytes: *T cells* and *B cells*. Both kinds are produced in the bone marrow. B cells are the ones that eventually produce the antibodies we have just discussed. In chickens, these cells mature in a structure called the bursa of fabricius (hence the "B" in B cells), and in animals such as ourselves they appear to mature in the bone marrow. The T cells, of which there are several different types, mature in the thymus gland (hence the initial "T"). We shall consider only two types of T cells in this chapter.

Rather early in the study of the immune system, it was found that the production of antibodies depended upon the presence of certain T cells from the thymus. Today these cells are called *helper T cells* because they help a B cell produce antibodies by attaching to the antigen and to the B cell. Helper T cells may also increase antibody production without attaching to B cells directly. In some cases, they may produce and release chemicals into the blood that cause the B cells to be activated or to reproduce. Without the participation of this class of T cells in at least one of these ways, how-

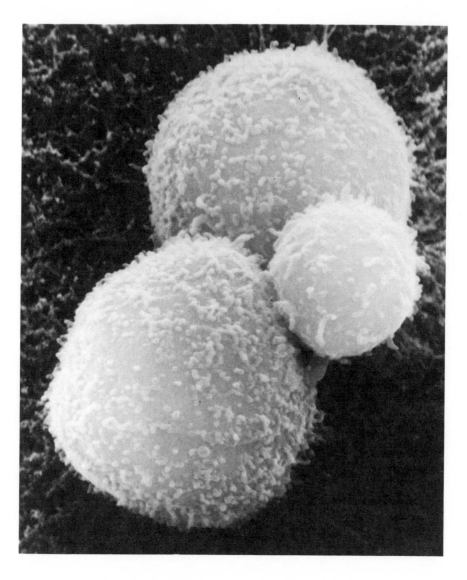

A scanning electron microscope shows an immune-system T-lymphocyte cell (the small one) attacking two large tumor cells.

ever, antibodies will not be produced. Helper T cells are sometimes also called T4 cells, because of a chemical found on their surfaces.

The second type of T cell that we shall consider is called a *suppressor T cell*. Suppressor T cells appear to be important in preventing the immune system from attacking the person's own tissues. They do this by suppressing, or keeping down the number of, helper T cells. All of this is part of the complex mechanism by which the immune system is able to attack foreign antigens and yet not attack the body's own cells. Suppressor T cells are sometimes called Ts cells (the "s" stands for "suppressor"), or T8 cells, again named after a chemical found on their surfaces.

3

TRANSMISSION

HOW DO YOU GET AIDS?

Some of you may find parts of this chapter upsetting or distasteful. In order to understand how AIDS is transmitted from one person to another, however, it is helpful to understand some things about sexual relationships. By writing about these we are not intending to show either approval or disapproval of them. However, we cannot stick our heads in the sand and pretend that certain behaviors we may not approve of simply do not occur. It is important to understand that AIDS is most commonly a *sexually transmitted* disease. In this chapter we will consider how it is transmitted between people. We will also look at how it is *not* transmitted between people.

In order for a person to get AIDS, there must be direct contact—an exchange of body fluids from an infected person to an uninfected person. In some diseases only one organism is needed for the infection to get started. Other diseases become established only if very large numbers of organisms, perhaps in the hundreds of thousands, invade the body at the same time. AIDS seems to be of this second type. Although the virus is found in many different body fluids, infection appears to occur only when there is a direct exchange of blood or semen.

Exchange via the blood can occur whenever a reasonably large volume of blood (containing many virus particles) is transferred from one person to another. Hemophiliacs, who are people that suffer from uncontrolled bleeding because their blood does not clot properly, receive frequent blood transfusions or injections of clotting factors derived from blood. Early in the appearance of AIDS in the United States, a number of hemophiliacs became infected with the disease. This was apparently a result of receiving blood or blood products donated by people who had the virus in their blood (and probably did not know it). Hemophiliacs also receive injections of something called Factor VIII, a part of the blood important in the clotting reactions that stop bleeding. These injections include Factor VIII from the blood of many different donors, increasing the chances that it may contain HIV. In early 1985, tests for the virus became available. Since that time, the entire blood supply in blood banks has been screened, and all newly donated blood is screened. Thus, it is extremely unlikely that anyone will get AIDS in this way in the future.

Another group who get AIDS directly from the transfer of blood are intravenous drug users. (Here, by the way, we are referring to users of *illegal* drugs, not people who receive regular medical injections of drugs such as insulin, cortisone, etc.) These people often get together in groups to share their drugs. They put all of the available drug into one syringe and needle and then pass the syringe from one person to the next. This is actually a very efficient way of transmitting AIDS. When a person sticks the needle into a vein, he or she usually draws a small amount of blood back into the syringe, to be sure that the needle is really in the vein. A little blood remains

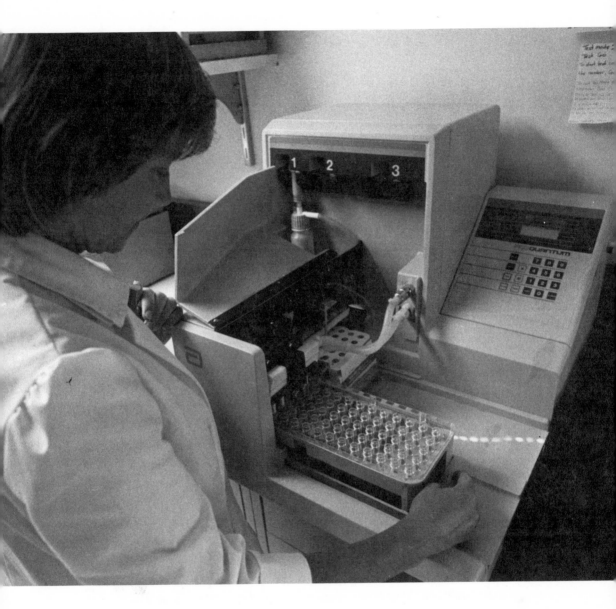

*A lab worker tests donated blood for AIDS
antibodies at a blood bank in Denver.*

in the syringe after the drug is injected. When the next person in the group follows this procedure, there is a good chance that some of the blood from the person who used it earlier will be injected. The third user may get infected blood from either of the first two, and so on.

The other major route by which the virus is transferred from one person to another is via semen. Semen is the mixture of fluids produced by males in their testicles and other sex glands. Men who have the AIDS virus in their blood also have a high concentration of the virus in their semen. Intercourse is said to occur when the penis is inserted into a woman's vagina. Semen is released from the penis during a process called ejaculation. If a woman has intercourse with a man who has the AIDS virus (even if he does not show any symptoms yet), the woman can become infected with the virus. During sexual intercourse, very small abrasions (cuts and scrapes) may be made in the wall of the vagina. These may serve as the route for entry for the virus. It also seems possible (though this author has not yet seen it suggested by anyone studying the disease) that if intercourse occurred during, or close to, the time at which a woman menstruates, entry to the woman's blood might be gained through the lining of the uterus, which bleeds at this time each month.

Sexual relationships between male homosexuals often involve *anal intercourse*. This is a type of sex in which semen is deposited by one man (called the "active partner") in the rectum of the other man (called the "passive partner"). If the active partner has the AIDS virus in his semen, then the passive partner is even more likely to become infected with the virus than are women who have normal sexual intercourse with an infected man. There are two reasons for this. One is that women are generally more resistant to infection than men are. The other reason is that the rectum is at the end of the large intestine. The large intestine is designed to absorb water.

The properties that make the large intestine able to absorb water efficiently also appear to make it able to absorb the virus deposited there by the semen. Water (and viruses) appear able to cross from the interior of the intestine to the blood rather easily, by way of blood vessels close to the inner lining of the large intestine.

There is one more factor that makes semen a good vehicle for the transfer of the AIDS virus. One of the normal functions of semen is to suppress the immune response of the female reproductive system. This prevents the female from rejecting the sperm in semen as a foreign material (an infection). Without this, pregnancies would never occur, and our species would not continue. It seems possible that this suppression of the immune response aids in the entry of the AIDS virus into the blood of women, through the vagina and, perhaps, the uterus. It may also aid its entry into the blood of passive male homosexual partners through the large intestine.

So far, we have seen that the AIDS virus can be transmitted from one person to another by the direct transfer of blood or by the transfer of semen. Two other routes of transmission may also occur. Women who have the AIDS virus may also transmit it to men. There are no glands in a woman's vagina that might secrete fluids containing the virus. During intercourse, however, when a woman becomes sexually excited, fluid passes from the blood to the vagina. This happens because of the increased blood flow and increased blood pressure in the surrounding vessels. In normal sexual activity this fluid lubricates (moistens) the vagina. This transfer of fluid, however, is not too different from that occurring across the large intestine, except that it is in the opposite direction. It seems likely that the AIDS virus is carried from the blood to the vagina along with the fluid produced. The virus may enter the man's body through his penis, but the details of how this happens are not yet understood.

At present, it is not clear how likely it is that a person of either sex will be infected by the AIDS virus as a result of one act of intercourse. There is some evidence to suggest that AIDS infection may be much more likely if the recipient has another sexually trans-mitted disease (STD), especially if it is one that causes open sores.

The last route by which a person can get AIDS is to be born to a mother who has the virus in her blood. In humans, the fetus (unborn baby) gets all of its oxygen, water, and nutrients from its mother. The transfer from mother to fetus occurs across an organ called the *placenta*. In the placenta, there are two beds of very fine blood vessels (the capillaries), where the blood from the mother comes very close to the blood of the fetus. Sometimes these capil-laries burst, and the blood of the mother and child come into direct contact. This appears to be the route by which the fetus gets the AIDS virus from an infected mother. The baby is born with AIDS and, because the immune system of newborns is not fully devel-oped, the child usually dies within the first year of life.

NONTRANSMISSION

All of what we said sounds pretty depressing. AIDS seems to be a disease that is easily transferred from one person to the next. If you

AIDS babies are often rejected by society, though they are not contagious. Here members of a religious order take care of several, who regularly play with David (on the right), a healthy twenty-one-month-old youngster adopted by the order.

mix blood or have intimate sex with someone who is infected, your chances of getting the disease are quite high. Most worrisome is the fact that it is not always possible to tell who has the virus and who does not.

For the moment, let us put aside the question of how a person can get the disease and consider how people do *not* get AIDS. We indicated earlier that the AIDS virus is found in many types of body fluids and secretions. It is found, for example, in both tears and saliva. However, *neither* of these fluids has been shown to serve as a route for transmission in anyone. Probably the best evidence of how difficult it is to get this disease from ordinary contact is taken from a study of the family members of AIDS victims. Being sneezed upon by someone with AIDS; sharing food, cups, towels, razors, and even toothbrushes; and kissing have all been done without transmission of the AIDS virus. There have been instances of children being bitten by other children who had AIDS, and infection has not occurred. Health workers (aides, nurses, and doctors) who care for AIDS patients have been exposed to the patients' blood, stool (feces), and urine and have even been vomited on. Of some 2,500 health care people who have been studied, three have become infected with the HIV virus as a direct result of an accident in which they stuck themselves with a needle containing blood freshly drawn from an AIDS patient. Three others apparently became infected after contact with blood through breaks in their skin.

The general message from studies of all the people who work with the disease and of those who deal daily with AIDS patients is that *AIDS is hard to get.* The organism appears to be extremely fragile. It survives only in blood and body secretions. It appears to be destroyed in normal passage through the digestive system. It does not live outside the body for very long, and infective organisms cannot be obtained from toilet seats or cooking or eating utensils. It shares all of these properties with other organisms that are considered to be sexually transmitted. Diseases are classified as sexually transmitted when that is the usual route by which they pass from one person to another. Most of these organisms are "fastidious"; that is, they survive and grow only in the male and female reproductive tracts. Most other sexually transmitted diseases are fastidious also and usually don't do much damage, but they can be difficult to get rid of.

Until AIDS came along, syphilis was probably the most serious of the STDs. Untreated, syphilis can lead to severe mental illness and death. Recently, it has been found that an STD known as *Chlamydia* has become quite common. It has few symptoms, but it can cause sterility (an inability to have children) in women if it is not treated promptly. Herpes, an STD caused by a virus, produces painful sores that appear unpredictably, but it seems to cause no serious problems for most of the people who have it. Like the organisms causing these diseases, the AIDS virus is spread mainly by direct sexual contact. Unlike most STDs, AIDS is fatal.

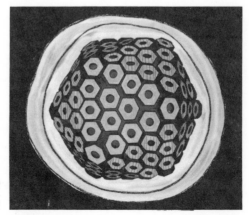

An illustration of the herpes simplex virus

Another problem occurs in some people who have the virus but do not yet have AIDS. For some reason, the virus sometimes attacks the brain, causing mental illness. Something similar happens with the several types of herpes viruses. One of these, *Herpes zoster,* causes chicken pox. After the skin eruptions disappear, the virus "hides out" in the nervous system. It may lie dormant there for a very long time. Later, the virus again becomes active and produces an extremely painful inflammatory condition known as *shingles.* With shingles, however, the virus attacks the nervous system outside the brain. Why the herpes and AIDS viruses enter the nervous system and why they lie dormant and then become troublesome later is not known.

CHAPTER
4

THE AIDS VIRUS

What is a virus? Ordinarily, we think of things as being either living or nonliving. We have no trouble agreeing that rocks, sand, air, and water are nonliving and that plants and animals are living organisms.

Protozoa, which are one-celled creatures, are about the smallest organisms consisting of true cells. Bacteria are smaller and simpler than the single-celled protozoa. Viruses are smaller and simpler than bacteria. They hardly resemble true cells at all. They consist of a package of genetic material, surrounded by a coat of protein, and they are completely dependent upon the cells they infect for their reproduction.

Most viruses consist of an outer coating of protein that surrounds the genetic material of the virus. Genetic material consists of chemically coded messages that are used for the production of a new organism. Usually the genetic material is DNA (*deoxyribonucleic acid*) and is located in the nuclei (central cores) of cells. When the DNA of a sperm (a male reproductive cell) and an egg (a female reproductive cell) combine, the development of a new person begins. The new cell includes all of the genetic material from both needed to direct the growth of the organism. Another way of saying this is that the DNA contains a code for all of the information needed to produce a new individual.

Viruses are fundamentally different from cells. For its genetic material, a virus may have either DNA or a related chemical, RNA

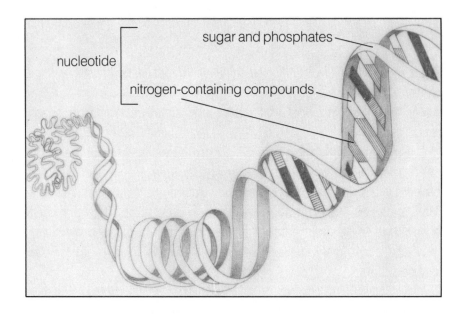

sugar and phosphates

nucleotide

nitrogen-containing compounds

Above: a section of the double-helix spiral strand of the human DNA code. Right: a strand of DNA within the cell, magnified 150,000 times and capable of harboring some 5,000 different amino acids

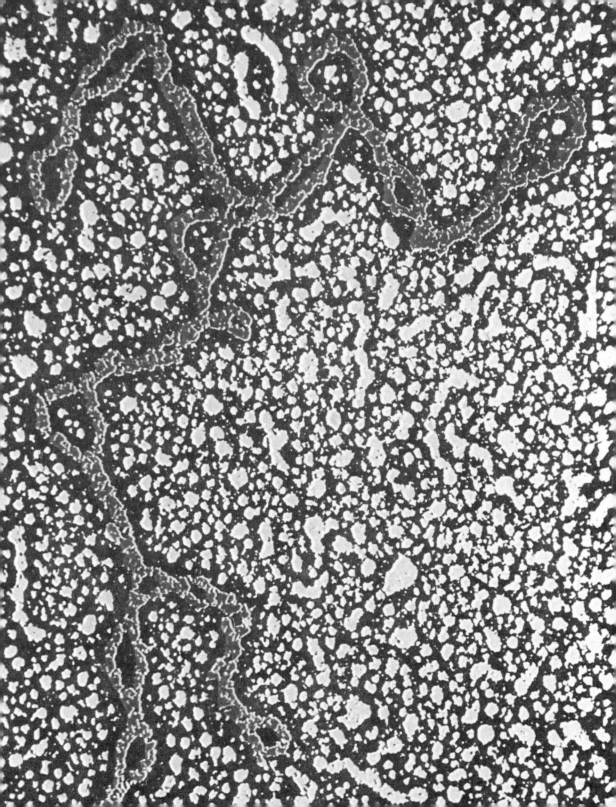

(*ribonucleic acid*). Viruses lack many of the materials needed to direct the production of new viruses. Instead, they attach to the surfaces of cells and inject their own DNA (or RNA) into the cell. There, the DNA or RNA "takes control of" part of the machinery of the cell and directs the synthesis of new viral DNA or RNA, plus the protein coat, for the production of new viruses.

The AIDS virus is a type of virus called a *retrovirus*. It uses RNA as its genetic material. The term refers to how these viruses produce their effects. We'll see how very soon.

For all cellular organisms, the information in DNA is decoded, or "read," in a certain way. Usually, the code in DNA is used to create an exact copy of that code in the form of RNA. The RNA is then used, or decoded, to produce proteins. Each of these substances—DNA, RNA, and protein—are long chains of molecules. DNA chains have four different kinds of links; RNA chains also have four different kinds of links (though they are slightly different from the links in DNA). The proteins have about twenty different kinds of links, called *amino acids*. The identity of the amino acids and the order of their arrangement serves as a sort of code, just as words are a sort of code made from the links (letters) of the alphabet. The use of the code in DNA to create a matching code in RNA is a process called *transcription*. The decoding of RNA to create a protein is called *translation*.

Now, you might recall that we said that the genetic material in the AIDS virus is RNA. It might be reasonable to assume that the RNA of this virus creates proteins directly, but this is not what happens. Instead, the RNA of the virus is used to create a matching code in DNA. This is the reverse of transcription (hence the name *retro*virus). Viruses of this type have an unusual enzyme (a type of protein that speeds up chemical reactions) that enables them to do

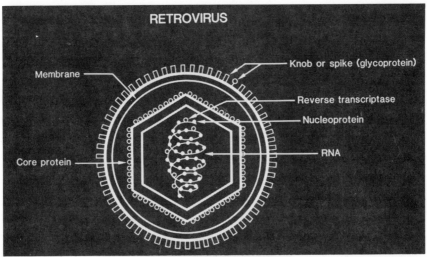

RETROVIRUS

Knob or spike (glycoprotein)

Membrane

Reverse transcriptase

Nucleoprotein

Core protein

RNA

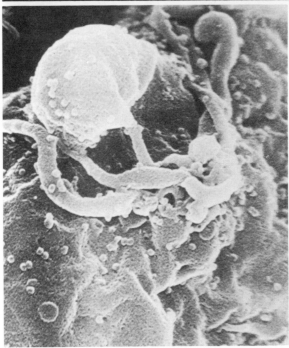

Above: a schematic of a retrovirus. Left: a scanning electron microscope reveals AIDS-infected T4 lymphocytes. The virus can be seen budding from the plasma membrane of the lymphocytes.

this. Because the process is the reverse of the usual process of converting DNA to RNA (transcription), this enzyme was given the name *reverse transcriptase*. After the virus has used this enzyme to produce DNA, the enzymes normally present in the cell cause the viral DNA to produce the usual sequence of RNA and protein. (These same enzymes perform the same job for the cells' own DNA). But the RNA and the protein are viral. In this way, the virus directs the cell to produce more of the virus. When a large amount of virus has been produced, the cell is destroyed and the virus is released into the bloodstream. There it encounters other cells, and the process starts all over again.

In AIDS, the virus attacks just one kind of cell. This type belongs to the class of immune system cells called *white blood cells,* or *leukocytes.* There are many different kinds of leukocytes. Some are lymphocytes (discussed in Chapter 2), and the type of cell attacked by the AIDS virus is the type of lymphocyte called the helper T cell, or T4. Helper T cells play a very important role in fighting disease. When they are destroyed, the ability of the body to fight disease is greatly reduced. The body may even become unable to recognize and destroy some of its own cells when they become abnormal. This results in cancers and is why people with AIDS die either by getting an infectious disease or from cancer.

CHAPTER

5

PROJECTIONS

Early in 1987, *U.S. News & World Report* published a large article on the subject of AIDS and addressed many questions people have regarding it. As we mentioned earlier, it appears that AIDS started in central Africa, perhaps ten or twenty years ago. The reasons for thinking it started in Africa are that (1) it appears to be most widespread there, and (2) its appearance in Europe and in the United States seems to trace back to Africa. AIDS appears to have entered Europe via a few men who became infected with the virus during trips to Africa and then infected women in their own countries.

The course of the disease in the United States is a bit unusual because it first appeared in the male homosexual community. In the beginning, many people who were not homosexual felt that AIDS would never affect them and that there was no reason to be concerned for their own health. In the United States, AIDS was spread to the heterosexual community by male and female IV drug users and by men who were bisexual (see Chapter 6). Once the virus

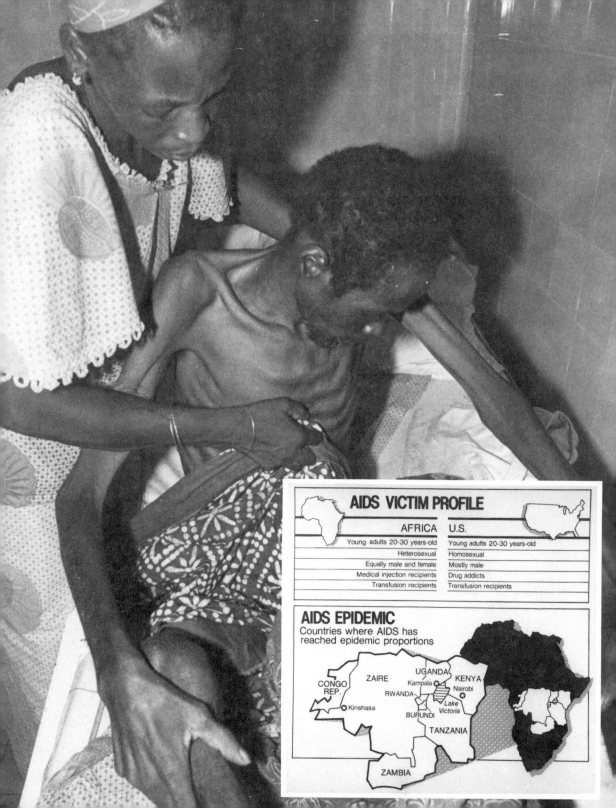

AIDS VICTIM PROFILE

AFRICA	U.S.
Young adults 20-30 years-old	Young adults 20-30 years-old
Heterosexual	Homosexual
Equally male and female	Mostly male
Medical injection recipients	Drug addicts
Transfusion recipients	Transfusion recipients

AIDS EPIDEMIC
Countries where AIDS has
reached epidemic proportions

CONGO REP.
ZAIRE
UGANDA
Kampala
KENYA
Nairobi
RWANDA
Kinshasa
Lake Victoria
BURUNDI
TANZANIA
ZAMBIA

infected heterosexual men and women, then most of the adult population in the country became vulnerable to the virus. In Africa, where it appears AIDS started, men and women are equally affected. As the disease spreads in the United States, the number of women with the disease could begin to approach the number of men infected.

Worldwide, there is far more sex between men and women than there is between homosexual couples. This means that the entire adult population of the world is now in danger. Infectious diseases can spread very rapidly, although they seem to start slowly. The rate of spread of such diseases is said to be *exponential.*

Probably the best way to show what this means is to illustrate with a very old question: "If someone offered you the chance to earn $10,000 a day each day for the next month, *or* the chance to earn one penny ($0.01) today, two pennies tomorrow, four pennies the next day, and so on, doubling the amount you earn each day for a month, which would you choose?" Let's see why you should take the penny doubling each day, even if the month were February, the shortest month of the year (twenty-eight days):

*Inset: AIDS victims on
the African continent,
as of mid-1986
Facing: an AIDS-stricken
African man is tended to
by his wife. The man is
thirty-five years old.*

	FIRST CHOICE ($10,000.00/day)		SECOND CHOICE (doubling each day)	
Day	Earned that day	Total	Earned that day	Total
1	$10,000.00	$ 10,000.00	$ 0.01	$ 0.01
2	$10,000.00	$ 20,000.00	$ 0.02	$ 0.03
3	$10,000.00	$ 30,000.00	$ 0.04	$ 0.07
4	$10,000.00	$ 40,000.00	$ 0.08	$ 0.15
5	$10,000.00	$ 50,000.00	$ 0.16	$ 0.31
6	$10,000.00	$ 60,000.00	$ 0.32	$ 0.63
7	$10,000.00	$ 70,000.00	$ 0.64	$ 1.27
8	$10,000.00	$ 80,000.00	$ 1.28	$ 2.55
9	$10,000.00	$ 90,000.00	$ 2.56	$ 5.11
10	$10,000.00	$100,000.00	$ 5.12	$ 10.23
11	$10,000.00	$110,000.00	$ 10.24	$ 20.47
12	$10,000.00	$120,000.00	$ 20.48	$ 40.95
13	$10,000.00	$130,000.00	$ 40.96	$ 81.91
14	$10,000.00	$140,000.00	$ 81.92	$ 163.83
15	$10,000.00	$150,000.00	$ 163.84	$ 327.67
16	$10,000.00	$160,000.00	$ 327.68	$ 655.35
17	$10,000.00	$170,000.00	$ 655.36	$ 1,310.71
18	$10,000.00	$180,000.00	$ 1,310.72	$ 2,621.43
19	$10,000.00	$190,000.00	$ 2,621.44	$ 5,242.87
20	$10,000.00	$200,000.00	$ 5,242.88	$ 10,485.75
21	$10,000.00	$210,000.00	$ 10,485.76	$ 20,971.51
22	$10,000.00	$220,000.00	$ 20,971.52	$ 41,943.03
23	$10,000.00	$230,000.00	$ 41,943.04	$ 83,886.07
24	$10,000.00	$240,000.00	$ 83,886.08	$ 167,772.15
25	$10,000.00	$250,000.00	$ 167,772.16	$ 335,544.31
26	$10,000.00	$260,000.00	$ 335,544.32	$ 671,088.63
27	$10,000.00	$270,000.00	$ 671,088.64	$1,342,177.27
28	$10,000.00	$280,000.00	$1,342,177.28	$2,684,354.55

Notice that the second choice does not make as much in one day as the first choice does until the end of the third week. Notice also that the second total does not exceed that of the first until the twenty-fifth day. Yet the second choice ends up with nearly ten times as much money as the first just three days later.

To understand how AIDS spreads, just substitute an infected person for each of the pennies earned by the second choice. At first, the numbers do not seem very impressive. But when the numbers become bigger, the amount of money earned becomes very impressive indeed.

Fortunately, the number of people with AIDS does not double every day. Early after its discovery in the United States, however, when it was still mostly confined to the homosexual population, it more than doubled each year. Many homosexual men have changed their life styles, however, and the disease is not spreading as rapidly as it was. As we noted earlier, however, the disease has now spread to the heterosexual population. The table below shows the number of cases of AIDS in the United States that have been reported and are expected during the ten years following the recognition of the disease.

Year	Number of Cases Reported or Expected	
1981	336	reported
1983	4,096	reported
1985	19,000	reported
1986	35,000	estimated
1988	91,000	estimated
1989	136,000	estimated
1990	194,000	estimated
1991	268,000	estimated

We are now about halfway through the first decade since the disease was reported. It is estimated that in the next five years there will be about ten times as many cases of AIDS in the United States as there are now. Unless a cure is discovered, half of these people will die within two years of being diagnosed. Five years from now, more people will have died of AIDS than died in the Korean and Vietnam wars combined.

Perhaps more frightening than these numbers is the estimate by the Centers for Disease Control in Atlanta, Georgia, that 1.5 million people now carry the virus but show no symptoms. Some people working with AIDS think that as many as 4 million people may be infected with the virus. It is possible that all of these people will develop AIDS. It is almost certain that from 25 to 50 percent will do so. If the lower estimates are right, this means that 375,000 of these people will die of AIDS. If the higher estimates are right, then 2 million people will die.

Until recently, all of the estimates made had seemed to be too conservative. More people caught AIDS than were expected to. And a larger fraction of the people with the virus had gone on to get AIDS than were expected to do so. But lately, according to some groups' calculations, the virus does not appear to be spreading as rapidly as had been feared, especially to the heterosexual community, perhaps because of changes in life style brought on by fear of the disease. If this is true, it is certainly good news, but it is too early to know if the slowdown is genuine and, if it is, whether it will continue.

It is distressing to learn that college and high school students in the United States—people who are young and beginning to be sexually active, and who should be well educated—do not seem to consider AIDS a serious threat to themselves. One of the curious traits of human beings is that we always seem to feel that misfortune happens to the "other guy." This general feeling of "it won't happen to me" is probably at its strongest when we are young adults, full of energy and with our whole lives in front of us. We just can't imagine that anything as awful as AIDS will happen to us. This is what the 30,000 people who have already died from the disease thought. This is what the 1.5 million or more people who are infected with the virus but don't know it yet still think, even though up to half of them will probably die of the disease. For all of these people, warnings—and vaccines, if they are ever developed—are already too late.

It is not too late for you. Dr. David Baltimore, who won the Nobel Prize in 1975 for his work on retroviruses, fears that young adolescents such as yourselves may be one of the most important groups to reach with information about AIDS. Obviously, reaching this group is the goal of this book.

CHAPTER

6

CURE AND PREVENTION

As stated earlier, there is presently no cure for AIDS and there is no vaccine to protect people against it. The more we learn about the AIDS virus and related viruses, the less likely it seems that a single vaccine will ever be found that protects against this disease. This is because the virus seems to exist in many different forms (possibly as many as a hundred). A different vaccine might be needed for each form of the virus.

If there is no cure and no vaccine, does that mean that we are all doomed? Of course not, just as we are not all destined to get a cold just because someone else in the room or in our family has one. Several hundred years ago, bubonic plague (the "Black Death") killed one out of four people in Europe. More recently, many people caught polio. Even before these diseases were brought under control, there were many who did not "catch" the disease. Apparently these people had a natural resistance to these diseases, just as some infectious organisms have a natural resistance to certain antibiotics such as penicillin.

You might recall from our earlier discussion that the AIDS virus must invade a healthy person in large numbers before it can establish an infection. There have been mothers who have given birth to infants who had AIDS, even though the mother was diagnosed (for up to three years after the birth of the child) as not having the disease.

Although it may be reassuring for the future of the human race that many people will be immune to the disease, it is not reassuring to learn of the very large number of people who are not immune and to risk the chance that you are one of them. How can a person avoid AIDS?

The answer is easy to say and, like most things, harder to do. The general answer is that a person should try to avoid actions that make it likely that he or she will be exposed to the disease. Don't have sex with someone who has AIDS. Don't have sex with men who are homosexual or bisexual (men who have sex with both women and men). Don't have sex with large numbers of partners. Don't have sex with people who have many other partners. Don't use illegal drugs.

The don'ts concerning sex may not be so easy to follow. Most of the readers of this book are just entering adolescence and becoming interested in (for the vast majority) the opposite sex.

Just what is safe, sexually speaking? Some frank discussion is in order here. There is really no way to be 100 percent sure of being safe except by avoiding all intimate contact with other people. If everyone avoided intimate relationships with members of the opposite sex throughout their lives, however, there would be no new births, and the human race would end with the present generation.

If all men and women had intimate sexual relationships with only one member of the opposite sex, the spread of AIDS would stop completely. Some religious and parents' groups argue that this is the only message that should be given to young people. Most people argue, however, that this is not likely to occur, given human nature and current standards of morality. Choosing a lifelong mate from the very start is difficult at best. Thus, it is better to be informed of other preventive measures, should the need arise, and to use them if there is even the slightest possibility of infection.

Sexually transmitted diseases are passed from infected people to those who are not infected most often when an infected person has sex (intercourse) with an uninfected person. Most people would not expose themselves to such a disease if they could tell that their partner had it. Unfortunately, it is not usually possible to tell if someone has the disease in the earlier stages. Until symptoms begin to show, most people who have the disease will not even know that they have it.

Who is most likely to have this disease, and why? As we have seen, one of the groups of people most likely to have it are male homosexuals, men who have sex with other men. There are several reasons why this is so. First, as we have seen, anal intercourse (insertion of the penis into the rectum) provides an easy route for the AIDS virus to enter the blood from the semen. Second, the life styles of many male homosexuals are unusual in that they may have very large numbers of partners in a very short time. Some may have as many as five thousand different partners within three years. This gives any STD a tremendous opportunity to expand throughout the population. Third, people who have at least one STD often have more than one, because they are all transmitted at once between new partners. The presence of other diseases may make people more likely to pick up the AIDS virus. Or, the AIDS virus may become active in a person who has already been infected with another STD.

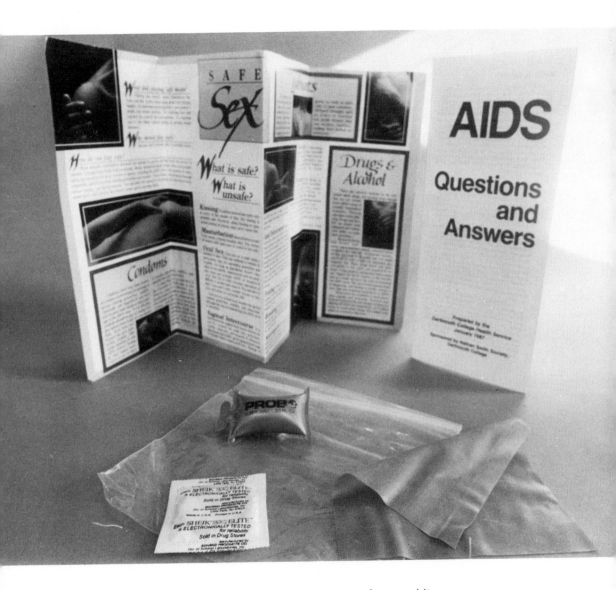

Shown here are the contents of a sex kit given to students at Dartmouth College to promote safe sex practices.

Intravenous drug users are also likely to have AIDS, as we have seen. Anyone in a group sharing the same needle may infect those who use the needle after him or her. Also, people who use illegal, addictive drugs heavily often fail to eat well or to take good care of themselves in other ways and so they are often in poor health. People in poor health are always at increased risk of getting infectious diseases, including AIDS.

A third group likely to have AIDS are female prostitutes, women who have sex with men for money. Like some male homosexuals, they usually have many different partners, and so they are exposed to many different kinds of STDs and other diseases. If any of their partners (customers) has AIDS, there is a significant chance that they will become infected with the AIDS virus. Of course, they may then pass it on to other men. If these men then have sex with other women, there is a significant chance the women will get it, and so on. In addition, many female prostitutes are intravenous drug users, increasing their chances of getting the disease that way.

Obviously, those at greatest risk of getting the disease seem to be those who have many different sexual partners. As far as STDs are concerned, when you have sex with someone you are also "having sex" with all of the people who have had sex with that person, with all of the people who have had sex with him or her, and so on. Just as obviously, people who do not have sex with anyone and who do not use intravenous drugs are the least at risk.

Most of the readers of this book do not have AIDS right now. During the teenage years, however, most people begin to experiment with sex, and in spite of warnings, some will have sexual relationships, homosexual and heterosexual. How can such a person keep his or her chances of exposure to the AIDS virus low?

The most obvious way is to severely limit the number of sexual partners. Also, sex with people who have had many partners should be avoided.

There are some methods that will make it less likely that the disease will be transmitted during intercourse. One of these seems to be for the man to use a *condom*. A condom, or "rubber," is a device that fits snugly over the penis so that semen is trapped and does not touch the partner's body. These devices, sold in all drugstores, if used properly offer good protection against pregnancy and sexually transmitted diseases. (Some religious groups oppose the use of condoms because they are a method of birth control.)

Other methods may offer some protection. Women may use *diaphragms,* which are devices that prevent semen from entering the uterus from the vagina. (Diaphragms must be fitted by a doctor.) Diaphragms used with a spermicidal (sperm-killing) cream or jelly, and contraceptive creams, foams, and jellies appear to kill the AIDS virus as well as sperm cells. But their effectiveness in preventing the spread of the disease is not known. At present, it appears that the condom gives the best protection against transmitting (or receiving) the AIDS virus.

Finally, once more, we must all acknowledge that there is no such thing as 100 percent safety. Part of the purpose of this book is to provide information that is helpful in letting the reader determine what is, and what is not, important to consider in avoiding this terrible disease. If we can limit the spread of AIDS by education and by care in our individual sexual behaviors, then it is more likely that a medical (drug) cure or vaccine will be developed before too many more people die of AIDS.

CHAPTER

7

SOCIAL ISSUES

AIDS will probably be of concern to you for the rest of your life. This is so because of two rather unusual features of the disease. First, AIDS is, as of now, 100 percent fatal. If you have full-blown AIDS, you almost surely will die of it, unless an effective treatment is found. Second, the people who can transmit AIDS to you may show no signs of the disease for years and may be completely unaware that they are carrying the infection and transmitting it to others.

Society is already grappling with the social consequences of AIDS. Since the disease is so serious and can be kept from spreading by identifying those who have it, should we test everyone for it? How dangerous is nonsexual contact with people who have full-blown AIDS? How is the practice of homosexuality to be viewed, considering the strong link between AIDS and homosexuality in this country? How can a person find a sexual or marriage partner without risk? How should a woman react when a man refuses to use a condom? These are just a few of the questions we must confront because of the AIDS epidemic. Some have been touched on al-

*Condoms and other contraceptives
line the wall in this drugstore.*

An AIDS worker consoles the sexual partner
and close friend of an AIDS victim. The friend
is also very likely to develop the disease.

ready in this book. We will explore some additional questions here, though it is very difficult to give definitive answers.

Why not test everyone for AIDS? This seems like the obvious thing to do. With tests we should eventually be able to identify everyone who has the disease and is likely to transmit it to others. But let's stop and think a minute. Is it really necessary to test everyone, even children only a year old and the very elderly, perhaps those past the age of ninety-five? If the answer is "no," then what ages should we exclude? Children under five? Ten? Senior citizens? Keep in mind that a number of young children are sexually molested each year, and that some adults remain sexually active throughout their entire lives.

Suppose we decide to test everyone within a certain age range. Does that mean we test even people who object? Some people who are at very high risk of AIDS (for example, long-time sexual partners of people who already have AIDS) do not want to know if they have the virus or not. They would rather cling to the possibility that they do not have the virus than find out for certain. In the United States, where the rights and freedoms of individuals are protected by the Constitution and state and local laws, it would be virtually impossible, legally speaking, to force a person to be tested for AIDS against his or her will, unless, of course, the laws are changed. Note that a recent large-scale test planned by the Centers for Disease Control had to be scaled down because of the refusal of many people to be tested.

Suppose, for a moment, that the laws are changed and that everyone is tested. There would be little point in testing everyone if the results were not made public (another Constitutional problem—the individual's right to privacy). Many of the more responsible AIDS victims have stopped having sex, or unprotected sex, but what about

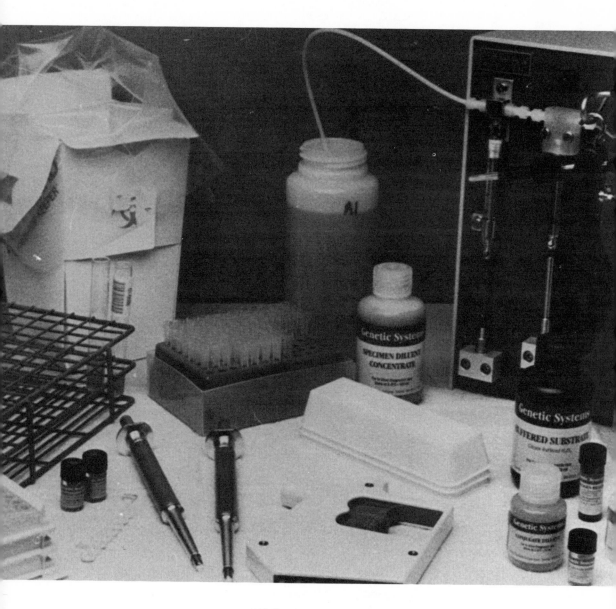

AIDS test components

the others? Furthermore, it would be necessary to test people repeatedly, since it is quite possible for a person to be infected and not show it, or become infected right after the test.

How often should testing be done, and who is going to pay for it? Should our government, through taxes, pay the bills?

Testing everyone will not be easy, and it will not provide any guarantees either. In the end, it may not be the best solution.

How dangerous is nonsexual contact with infected persons? This is easier to answer. You have probably heard about cases in which children with the AIDS virus were prevented from attending school. Sometimes, when they were allowed to attend, the parents of the other children kept their children at home. In almost every case, incidentally, these children had hemophilia.

What is the danger of catching AIDS from a classmate? A coworker? Should people with AIDS be isolated from society?

One of the few good things about AIDS is that it is hard to catch, as we said earlier. It requires direct contact and the direct exchange of bodily fluids. The family members of AIDS victims appear to be at little risk, and they live in close contact with the disease every day. There is little to fear from ordinary contact with a person who has this disease, and there seems little reason to even consider isolating the victims of the disease from society.

Since AIDS first took hold in the United States in the homosexual community, it was once thought that AIDS was a "homosexual" disease. Some people even suggested that AIDS is somehow a punishment for immoral or sinful behavior. Most news reports linked AIDS and homosexuality to such an extent that it is hard to make people understand the truth. As we have seen, however, in Africa AIDS is a heterosexual disease, spread from men to women and women to men.

AIDS education in the classroom.
In the end, education may be
our best hope in fighting the disease.

Homosexuality has never been widely accepted in most Western societies, and many people who view the practice as perverted or sinful actually try to blame homosexuals for having started the disease. As a result of the connection between AIDS and homosexuality, homosexuals are often subject to angry abuse, both physical and mental, from these people. AIDS victims often receive little sympathy for their condition, and become hated and feared outcasts of society.

These are just a few of the social issues related to AIDS that will be facing us in the times to come. For AIDS is not just another disease. Its seriousness must make us all stop and think—about our feelings for close friends, about our sexuality and sexual behavior, and about how much and in what ways we want society or government to intervene in our lives to help prevent its spread.

SUGGESTED READINGS

Benza, Joseph F., Jr., and Ralph D. Zumwalde. *Preventing AIDS: A Practical Guide for Everyone.* Jalsco Inc. Cincinnati, Ohio, 1986.

Frumkin, Lyn, and John Leonard. *Questions and Answers on AIDS.* Avon. New York, 1987.

Hall, Lynn, and Thomas Modl, eds. *AIDS.* Greenhaven Press. St. Paul, Minn., 1987.

Hyde, Margaret, and Elizabeth Forsythe. *AIDS: What Does It Mean to You?* Rev. ed. Walker. New York, 1987.

Jacobs, George, and Joseph Kerrins. *The AIDS File.* Cromlech Books, Inc. Woods Hole, Mass., 1987.

Martelli, Leonard J., et al. *When Someone You Know Has AIDS: A Practical Guide.* Crown Publishers, Inc. New York, 1987.

Nourse, Alan. *AIDS.* Franklin Watts, Inc. New York, 1986.

Silverstein, Alvin and Virginia. *AIDS: The Deadly Threat.* Enslow, New Jersey, 1986.

You can also call the AIDS Information Hotline, twenty-four hours a day, seven days a week, at 1-800-342-AIDS.

INDEX

AIDS researchers, 14
AIDS test components, 64
AIDS viruses identified, 14, 41-46
AIDS workers, 62
Amino acids, 44
Anal intercourse, 34
Antibiotics, 24
Antibodies, 24, 27
Antigens, 24
ARC (AIDS-related complex), 17, 19-20
Autoimmune diseases, 28
AZT, 22

Babies, as AIDS victims, 36, 37
Baltimore, David, 53
B cells, 28
Beginning of AIDS, 9-12. *See also* Africa
Birth control devices, 59, 61
Bisexual men and AIDS, 47
Blood banks, 32, 33
Blood, transmission of AIDS through, 32
Bone marrow, 24, 28

Cancer, 19, 20, 46. *See also* Kaposi's sarcoma
Cases, number of, 51-53
Centers for Disease Control, 52, 63
Chicken pox, 40
Children's exposure to AIDS, 38, 65
Chlamydia, 39
Condoms, to prevent AIDS, 59, 61
Connective tissue, 19
Contraceptive creams, foams, and jellies, to prevent AIDS, 59, 61
Contraceptives, 59, 61
Cure and preventive, 21-22, 54-59

Diaphragms, to prevent AIDS, 59

DNA, 41-44, 46
Donated blood, screening of, 32, 33
Double helix spiral strand of DNA code, 42
Drugs used in treatment of AIDS, 22

Education about AIDS, 59, 66
Enzymes, 44, 46
Essex, Myron, 14
Exponential diseases, 49

Factor VIII, 32
Families of AIDS victims, 38
Food and Drug Administration, 22

Gallo, Robert, 14, 16
Green monkey, AIDS in, 12, 13

Health workers' exposure to AIDS, 38
Helper T cells, 20, 28, 30, 46
Hemophiliacs, 32
Herpes simplex virus, 39
Herpes zoster, 40
Heterosexual community, spread of AIDS in, 47, 49
HIV virus, 15-16, 20
Homosexuality, public attitude towards, 65, 67
Homosexual men, as AIDS victims, 10, 12, 34, 47, 51, 56
HTLV-III virus, 15-16

Illegal drug use and spread of AIDS. *See* Intravenous drug users
Immune system, 16, 19, 20, 21, 23-30
Immunity to AIDS, 54-55
Infectious diseases, 24, 49
Intravenous drug users, 10, 32, 34, 47, 58

Kaposi's sarcoma, 9, 10, 19, 20